Mountains and Hills

Louise and Richard Spilsbury

Heinemann
LIBRARY

www.heinemann.co.uk/library
Visit our website to find out more information about **Heinemann Library** books.

To order:
☎ Phone 44 (0) 1865 888066
🖹 Send a fax to 44 (0) 1865 314091
💻 Visit the Heinemann Bookshop at www.heinemann.co.uk/library to browse our catalogue and order online.

First published in Great Britain by Heinemann Library, Halley Court, Jordan Hill. Oxford OX2 8EJ, part of Harcourt Education.

Heinemann is a registered trademark of Harcourt Education Ltd.

Editorial: Lucy Thunder and Helen Cannons
Design: David Poole and Kamae Design
Picture Research: Hannah Taylor and Liz Savery
Production: Edward Moore

Originated by P.T. Repro Multi-Warna
Printed and bound in Hong Kong and China by WKT Company Limited

The paper used to print this book comes from sustainable resources.

ISBN 0 431 12122 2 (hardback)
08 07 06 05
10 9 8 7 6 5 4 3 2

ISBN 0 431 12129 X (paperback)
09 08 07 06 05
10 9 8 7 6 5 4 3 2 1

British Library Cataloguing in Publication Data
Spilsbury, Louise and Spilsbury, Richard
Mountains and Hills – (Wild habitats of the British Isles)
577.5'3'0941
A full catalogue record for this book is available from the British Library.

Acknowledgements
The Publishers would like to thank the following for permission to reproduce photographs: Bruce Coleman Collection/John Cancalosi p**16**; Holt Studios p**17**; Jason Hawkes Aerial Photography Library p**24** bottom; John Cleare Mountain Camera Library p**18** bottom; London Aerial Photo Library p**6**; National Trust Photographic Library/Ian Shaw p**28**; Mark Boulton pp**10**, **12** bottom; NHPA/Alan Williams p**19**; NHPA/G J Cambridge p**15**; NHPA/Laurie Campbell p**23**; Ordnance Survey pp**12** top, **18** top, **24** top; Oxford Scientific Films/Barrie Watts p**21**; Oxford Scientific Films/Mark Hamblin p**29**; Oxford Scientific Films/Steve Littlewood p**7**; Simon Warner p**26**; Woodfall Wild Images p**14**; Woodfall Wild Images/D Woodfall pp**8**, **9**; Woodfall Wild Images/M Lane p**11**; Woodfall Wild Images/Mark Hamblin p**25**; Woodfall Wild Images/P&A Macdonald p**20**; Woodfall Wild Images/Peter Wilson p**13**; Woodfall Wild Images/Steve Austin p**22**; Woodfall Wild Images/Val Corbett p**4**.

Cover photograph of heather-covered moorlands, reproduced with permission of Woodfall Wild Images.

The Publishers would like to thank Michael Scott, wildlife consultant and writer, for his assistance in the preparation of this book.

Contents

Any words appearing in the text in bold, **like this**, are explained in the Glossary.

Mountain and hill habitats

Mountains usually rise high above the surrounding land and have a prominent, rugged peak. In the British Isles, most mountains reach over 500 metres above sea level, but in many other places around the world, mountains are much higher. Hills are usually more rounded and smaller than mountains. Any land over 300 metres above sea level is called **upland**.

Get this!

Around half of Britain is upland. Over half of all British mountains are in Scotland.

What is a mountain or hill habitat?

A **habitat** is the natural home of a group of **organisms**. Organisms are living things such as plants and animals. The habitat provides them with what they need to survive, such as food and shelter from bad weather.

Mountains and hills can be difficult places to live. The tops of the tallest mountains are often cloudy, windy, icy, wet and steep. Few organisms live on windswept crags of bare rock. More plants and animals live where they can find some shelter. For example, some plants live along the edges of rushing streams, in cracks in rocks or on gentle slopes. Some large areas of upland are covered with plants and rich in wildlife.

The Lake District is an area of mountains in north-west England. ➜

4

Life on uplands

Uplands are an important type of habitat in the British Isles. Many of the **species** that live there are **adapted** – specially suited – to the conditions. Some of these species used to live in lower land near by, or were widespread all over Britain. Today they survive in uplands partly because these areas provide the right habitat, but partly because they are wild places. Although there may be lots of visitors, few people want to live or work in the **exposed** conditions. This means there is less disturbance for animals and plants on upland than on lower land.

Interdependent life

The organisms in any habitat are interdependent – this means their lives are related. A simple upland example of this is grass and eagles. Eagles do not eat grass, but they do hunt animals, such as rabbits, that are grass-eaters. If there is not enough grass for rabbits to eat, then there will be fewer rabbits for eagles to eat. Organisms are interdependent in many different, often complex, ways.

Key
- 400m above sea level

Shetland Islands

North West Highlands

Grampians

N

Southern Uplands

Cumbrian Mts.

Mourne Mts.

Pennines

Cambrian Mts.

Brecon Beacons

Dartmoor

```
0          100 miles
0          100 km
```

← This map shows that most mountains and hills in the British Isles are in the north and west. An area with lots of mountains close together, sometimes in rows, is called a mountain range.

How do mountains and hills form?

The mountains and hills of the British Isles started to form millions of years ago. Some mountains formed because of volcanoes. Volcanoes are deep holes that open in the Earth's surface rock. Hot, melted rock inside the Earth erupts (spurts out) of these holes. As the rock cools it hardens. As more melted rock builds up on top of it over time, the sides of the volcano get taller, to form large hills or even mountains of rock. An example of volcanic hills is the Malvern Hills, south-west of Birmingham. These hills formed around 600 million years ago.

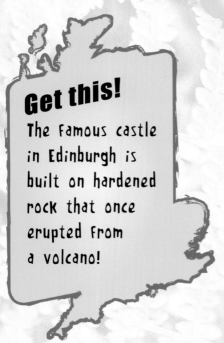

Get this!

The famous castle in Edinburgh is built on hardened rock that once erupted from a volcano!

Rock on the move

Although it is incredibly heavy, the hard rock of Earth's surface floats like huge rafts on the melted rock deep inside. Some British mountains first formed when large chunks of the surface rock floated into each other. Millions of years ago, when they collided together, rocks on the surface crumpled previously flat areas of land into hills and mountains.

The incredible forces pushing inside the Earth have buckled its surface. This has made mountains and hills. The Caledonian mountains formed 400 million years ago after surface rocks crumpled. ➔

6

Erosion

Although many hills and mountains began as jagged peaks, their shape has changed over millions of years because they are being worn away. This is called **erosion**. Erosion can happen when water, wind or ice gradually wears away surface rock. British hills and mountains are made of many different types of rock. Harder rocks erode much more slowly than softer rocks.

Weathering

Erosion also happens through **weathering**. For example, if rainwater that gets into tiny cracks in rock then freezes, it pushes open the cracks, breaking off small pieces of rock. The small pieces wear down further, sometimes with the help of tiny **organisms**, to eventually form soil.

In the past Dartmoor, in south-west England, was covered by sea! When the sea dried up, the mud at the bottom dried, forming a coating of softer rock over the hard volcanic rock underneath. Since then, wind and rain has eroded this softer rock in places, exposing rock peaks called tors, like this one. ↓

Life in limestone

Limestone is soft rock that is easily eroded by water. The cracks and grooves in large flat areas of exposed limestone – called pavement – provide sheltered, moist conditions where organisms, such as ferns, can thrive.

Changes on mountains and hills

The kinds of plants and animals you find on a mountain or hill change as you climb higher. This is because the higher up a mountain **organisms** grow and live, the more challenges they face. They are more **exposed** to strong winds, cold air and heavy rain.

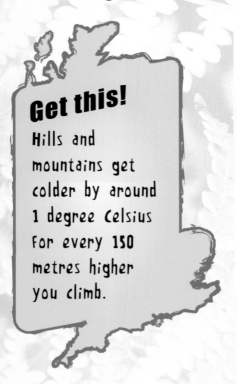

Get this!

Hills and mountains get colder by around 1 degree Celsius for every 150 metres higher you climb.

Zones of life

There are generally three **zones** (levels) of plants on hills and mountains. In the lowest zone there are usually lots of trees. However, this is not always obvious because people in the past have cleared forests so that they can use the land for farming or for building on. In the middle zone there are fewer trees, but lots of plants such as grass and heather. In the top zone it is too cold and windy and the soil is too thin for any trees to grow. There may be some plants that grow close to the ground, out of the path of icy winds.

Different species of plants on hills, such as the Cairngorms in Aberdeenshire, Scotland, grow at particular levels. The point at which trees stop growing on a mountain is called the tree line. →

← During cold winter weather, water often falls from clouds as snow on higher hills and mountains. Areas such as the North Yorkshire **moorland** are often cloaked in clouds for days on end.

Seasonal changes

The weather on mountains and hills changes with the seasons and this affects plant and animal life. In summer the weather is mainly warm and dry, and there are more hours of daylight. This is when most plants flower. **Insects** hatch from eggs or come out of **hibernation** to feed on the **nectar** in the flowers. As they do so they also help the plants by **pollinating** the flowers. Animals such as birds, which eat insects, come to the mountains and hills to feed and have their young. In winter, when it is wet and cold, there are few flowers and insects. Mountains are then much quieter places.

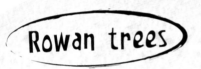

Rowan trees

Rowan trees – sometimes called mountain ash – are tough and can survive winter frosts. Rowan trees are short and have small leaves. In autumn they produce clusters of red berries. These berries are an important source of autumn food for birds such as thrushes, which eat the berries. Birds spread the **seeds** in their droppings.

This drawing of rowan leaves and their berries will help you to spot a rowan tree when you are out walking.

Life on wooded slopes

Woodlands grow on the lower slopes of many mountains and hills in the British Isles. Trees provide shelter for many animals and smaller plants that live amongst them.

Broadleaved trees

The lowest, most sheltered places on slopes are usually home to many **broadleaved** trees. In autumn, as the weather cools, the leaves of most broadleaved trees turn brown, yellow and red and fall off. The trees remain bare until the following spring when new leaves grow. Broadleaved trees in Britain include oak, ash and birch. Many small plants that grow on the woodland floor, such as bluebells, produce flowers in spring, before broadleaved trees fill out with leaves.

Animals among broadleaved woods

Lots of different animals live at different levels of woodland. Great spotted woodpeckers nest in holes high in trees. They drum their tough beaks against branches and trunks to find **insects** to eat under the bark. Badgers live in holes amongst tree roots. They come out at night to sniff out food, such as worms and snails.

The branches and leaves of broadleaved trees form a patchy roof over the ground – called a canopy – in spring and summer, shading the ground below. ↓

A birch tree habitat

A birch tree provides a mini-**habitat** for many different **organisms**. **Fungi** that live underneath it on the ground break down fallen birch leaves to release **nutrients**. Some of these nutrients are taken up through the roots of plants such as violets. Over 300 **species** of insect live on and eat the leaves and cracked bark of birch trees.

Conifer trees

Conifer trees can grow higher up a mountainside than broadleaved trees. Conifers have narrow, **waxy** leaves that can cope with colder and more **exposed** conditions. Conifers do not make their seeds in flowers, but instead in woody **cones**.

Some conifers, such as Scots pine, are **native** trees – they have grown in Britain for thousands of years. Others, such as sitka spruce, are not native. They were brought into this country and planted by people. Fewer animals and plants live on the floor beneath conifers because it is quite dark – the trees have a dense covering of leaves all year round.

↑ Siskins are small yellow-green birds that eat birch **seeds** in autumn. Their beaks have fine points to pick out seeds and broad bases to crush them.

11

Bredon Hill, England

Bredon Hill, near Evesham in Worcestershire, is a small hill reaching just over 250 metres above sea level. On Bredon Hill there are several areas of tall, ancient trees and also scrub. Scrub is made up of tangled, low-growing shrubs such as hawthorn and climbing plants. Much of the land is covered in grass and grazed by sheep over many decades.

↑ This map shows the location of the gentle slopes of Bredon Hill. Woodland areas are shown in green.

This photo of Bredon Hill shows the ancient ash trees growing there. One of the trees' large trunks has fallen, providing food and shelter for animals. →

Plant life

The main kind of grass that grows on Bredon Hill is upright brome. Upright brome has stems up to 1 metre tall and makes thousands of seeds in summer. A variety of other small plants grow amongst the brome. Pyramidal orchids emerge from their underground bulbs in early spring. Their pink flowers form a pyramid shape.

Butterflies

Grasses and other flowering plants attract a range of butterflies. Brown argus butterflies lay their eggs on rock rose plants. When the caterpillars hatch, they eat the plant's leaves. Once they change into butterflies, they eat flower **nectar**.

Scrubland birds

Different birds nest in the scrub at Bredon Hill. It is too tangled there for most **predators** to reach them. Male whitethroats make their nests out of grass and roots, often lined with sheep wool. The female lays about five glossy, blue-green eggs inside. The flowers and berries on climbing scrub plants such as honeysuckle and ivy attract many **insects** that these birds feed on.

Insects in ancient trees

The oldest trees at Bredon Hill, such as oak or ash, are over 300 years old. Old **native** trees are important **habitats** for many insects. They naturally rot on the inside over time forming hollow trunks. These trunks provide shelter and food – rotting wood – for beetles.

Violet click beetle

The violet click beetle is one of the rarest beetles in Britain. It has only been found at Windsor Forest, near London, and at Bredon Hill. It is not often seen in the open as it lives in the dark, rotting bases of hollow trunks of ancient trees, especially ash. Click beetles get their name from the clicking sound they make when they jump to their feet after falling over. 'Violet' is the colour of their shiny wing covers.

Heath and moorland plants

The middle zone of mountains and hills is often described as 'open' – that means there are not many trees around. Most of the plants that live there are small shrubs and strong grasses. This type of **habitat** is called heath. There are few **bacteria** in heath soils to break down dead heath plants, and release their **nutrients** back into the ground. This means that the soil is low in nutrients so many heath plants grow slowly.

Dry heath

Some heath remains dry because rainwater drains away into its sandy soil. Some of the plants that grow here include bilberry, heather and three different kinds of gorse. These are all tough, woody plants with small leaves.

Heather

One of the shrubs you are most likely to see on **upland** heath is heather. Heather leaves are coated in a shiny **wax** that helps stop them losing water. Heather makes its small, purple, bell-shaped flowers in the warmest parts of the year, when there are lots of **insects** around to **pollinate** them. It often takes around six years for heather to grow from **seed** to small bush, but it may live up to 30 years.

Wet moorland

Some areas of heath do not drain quickly because the rock underneath is very hard. This keeps some areas of soil wet most of the time. High, **exposed** and wet areas of heath are usually called **moorland**.

Moorland plants include grasses, heather and mosses. Sphagnum moss plants have lots of tiny leaves that trap water a bit like a sponge. This means mossy areas remain wet and form **bogs**. When sphagnum moss dies, what remains of it forms a spongy soil called **peat**.

Only a few plants other than peat grow in bogs because bogs are acidic. Dead plants rot even more slowly in this cold, acidic water, so most nutrients are trapped in layers of peat. In some areas the peat is up to five metres thick. The largest bogs in Britain are called blanket bogs. They cover areas measuring hundreds of square kilometres in northern Scotland.

Get this!

Heath and moorland covers over 20,000 square kilometres in the British Isles, and makes up around one-tenth of the world total.

← The sundew plant thrives in blanket bogs because the bogs attract flies – and the sundew eats flies! Sundew has special leaves covered in sticky hairs. When flies land on the leaves, they get stuck! The sticky fluid breaks down the flies to release nutrients for the plant.

Heath and moorland wildlife

Many types of wildlife live on **upland** areas of heath and **moorland**. These areas provide a range of places to live, from thick layers of shrubs to wet expanses of **bog**.

Life amongst the shrubs

Many small animals find food and shelter amongst the shrubs. Some feed on the leaves and berries of plants but others feed on the **insects** that live there. Heath tiger beetles are black with white stripes. They spot **prey** such as ants and caterpillars with their large eyes, and use their sharp jaws to catch a meal.

Red grouse nest on the ground amongst heather and bilberry shrubs. Grouse chicks avoid **predators**, such as foxes and **birds of prey**. They hide with the help of their speckled **camouflaged** feathers. Grouse eat insects when young, but move on to a diet of leaves and buds of bilberry and heather when adult. The whinchat is a small brown bird with apricot-coloured feathers underneath. It feeds on insects and berries among the shrubs.

Adders are Britain's only poisonous snakes. They can sometimes be seen in open patches amongst the shrubs, basking in the sun. They need to bask to soak up warmth from the sun before they can become active. ↓

Bog life

Many flies live around bogs. Craneflies are large flies that lay their eggs in wet soil or under moss plants. Cranefly **larvae** (young) – often called leatherjackets – eat plant roots but adults can only drink liquids. Biting midges are tiny flies that live in bogs. They lay their eggs in water and the larvae breathe underwater using tiny tubes. Adult females feed on the blood of large **mammals** such as ponies or humans! Adult males do not feed – they live just long enough to **mate** and then die.

Visiting birds

Many birds that live by British coasts in winter move on to moorland in spring and summer. They do this partly because these are quiet places to make their nests on the ground. Curlews feed their chicks on insects, snails and worms. They catch them amongst the bog grasses with their long, curved beaks.

Red deer

Red deer roam across Scottish moorland. They are the biggest upland animals in the British Isles. Red deer feed on grass during summer, and heather leaves during winter when the grass has died back. Males – called stags – rut (fight each other) in autumn. They push each other using their antlers. The winner mates with more females than the loser.

17

Snowdonia, North Wales

Snowdonia covers an area of over 2000 square kilometres (840 square miles) of North Wales. It includes several mountain ranges including the tallest mountain in Wales – Snowdon – and large areas of **moorland**.

The Migneint moorland on the Ysbyty Estate is covered with heather, coarse grasses and sedges. A sedge plant looks quite like a grass plant, but its stem is triangular not circular. At Migneint, purple moor grass forms thick clumps called tussocks. The outer leaves of each tussock protect the inner leaves from wind and cold.

Mammal runs

Many small **mammals** live amongst the thick grasses on the Migneint moorland. Voles are little **rodents** with short tails. They eat grass and also shred it to form nests at the base of tussocks. Voles travel along the same routes between tussocks and create paths as they trample the grass. Weasels are one of the most common **predators** in Britain. They have a long ginger-brown body with a cream underside. They hunt voles but also eat bird eggs, chicks and baby rabbits.

↑ This map shows part of Snowdonia. The closer together the red contour lines are, the steeper it is.

Migneint is a bleak area of rolling moorland in Snowdonia, Wales. ➔

18

Airborne hunters

The animals that live in and around moorland plants are a tempting meal for predators. **Birds of prey**, such as hobbies and merlins, hunt at Migneint. They have excellent vision and hearing to help find **prey**. They catch their food using sharp curved claws, which they use to hold the food while they rip it up using a hooked beak.

Hobbies are slim birds that glide low over the ground with their long wings. They often hunt over heather, catching large **insects** and rodents. Merlins are the size of a blackbird. They have grey backs and reddish feathers underneath. Merlins perch or hover before flying very fast to catch small birds and mammals.

Daytime owl

Most owls hunt at night, but short-eared owls (shown here) hunt voles and other mammals over Snowdonian moorland during the day. They eat the flesh of their prey, but parcel up the hair and bones they cannot digest in their stomach. They then spit out these parcels – called owl pellets – before they feed again.

Short-eared owls get their name from the tufts of feathers on their head. However, these are not ears! Short-eared owls raise the tufts when they feel threatened so other owls can see them.

Plants on mountain tops

Trees usually cannot grow at more than about 800 metres above sea level in Britain because it is so cold, dry and windy. The few plant **species** that do grow on mountain tops **adapt** to survive these conditions.

Life on bare rock

Most mountain plants need some soil to grow in, but lichens do not — they live on **exposed** bare rock. Lichens are very special **organisms** — they are partly plant and partly **fungi**. Tiny green plants in lichen make sugar through **photosynthesis**. They live inside tough fungi. The fungi form a shelter and help release **nutrients** from rocks for the plants. The plants provide the fungi with food. Neither can survive without the other.

Map lichens can be found on British mountains. They get their name from the black and yellow pattern they make on the rock, which looks a bit like a section of a map. Map lichens, like most other lichens, grow incredibly slowly — less than one millimetre each year.

The conditions at the top of a mountain are harsh for plants. There is often a lot of bare rock and not much soil. It is very exposed to extreme weather. ➔

20

Growing in sheltered places

Many mountain plants grow in sheltered cracks or grow in hunched-up shapes. Plants often grow on rock ledges because they are out of reach of sheep that would **graze** on them elsewhere. Mountain avens is a small straggly shrub. As it grows it gradually creeps along sheltered cracks in rocks. It stays put by anchoring itself using long roots. Its small leathery leaves are hairy underneath to trap any moisture from mists.

Many mountain-top plants, including mountain avens, produce large bright flowers for a short time in early summer. This is when mountain weather is warm enough for **insect pollinators** such as moths to be around.

Moss campion

Moss campion is a cushion-forming plant. It grows up to 15 centimetres tall and is found as high as 1300 metres above sea level. It huddles down to keep warm, and grows tightly packed in a cushion-shaped clump. This shape helps to shed water from the plant – to stop it becoming waterlogged in bad weather. It also prevents the thin bits of soil it grows on from blowing or washing away. Although the outer plants may be damaged by exposure to wind and cold, the plants in the middle of the cushion survive.

21

Wildlife of mountain tops

The **exposed** conditions on mountain tops mean many animals keep away. Apart from being windy and cold, there are few plants to feed on or to give shelter. Many small animals only come out for short periods when it is warm enough to be active.

Mountain ringlet butterflies

Some butterflies fly up to cold and high mountain slopes. Mountain ringlet butterflies are brown, hairy butterflies with small orange spots. They are only active in sunny weather. They usually lay their eggs on mat grass, a hardy mountain grass. In late summer, any **larvae** on the grass move down into the soil to spend autumn and winter there until it is warm enough to emerge.

Mountain-top mammals

Mammals that live on mountain tops keep warm using a thick coat of hair. Mountain hares have a short brown summer coat of hair. In autumn they moult – the summer hair falls out to be replaced by a thicker, white winter coat. In summer, the brown hares blend better with the brownish rocks they live amongst. Both these coats are used as **camouflage**.

This is a mountain hare with its thick white winter coat. When the ground is covered by snow, **predators**, such as golden eagles, are less likely to spot the white hare. ↓

In winter, mountain hares form large groups for safety in numbers. They scrape away the snow to uncover food, such as grass and heather, and to make sheltered places to rest in. While some are feeding, others keep a look out for danger.

Mountain-top birds

Some large birds live all year round on mountains. Ravens and golden eagles are both strong fliers in swirling winds. They both nest on rocky crags. Ravens look like very large crows, but with thicker black feathers under their beak. Their deep croaking call can be heard across mountains. Ravens feed on carrion – dead animals such as sheep and deer they find.

In late spring, quiet mountain tops attract visiting **breeding** birds. Dotterels are birds that spend winter in hot, dry places in African countries. They fly long distances to Britain to nest during the summer. They nest on the ground amongst lichen-covered boulders.

Golden eagles

Golden eagles are rare, enormous birds you might be lucky enough to see soaring near the tops of mountains. They spread their two-metre wide wings and glide in rising warm air above slopes. As they soar, they search for carrion and **prey**, such as red grouse and mountain hares, to catch and eat.

Grampian Mountains, Scotland

The Grampian Mountains run through the centre of Scotland from south-west to north-east. They are part of the Highlands of Scotland, which are so-named because they are made up of high mountain ranges. The rainwater that falls on these huge **uplands** collects in streams that feed into rivers, such as the River Spey, and lochs (lakes). A row of massive lochs, including Loch Ness, lies in the deep valley between the Grampians and the northern Highlands.

Caledonian Forest

Thousands of years ago large areas of Scotland were covered in forest called the Caledonian Forest. Today, there are only small patches of Caledonian Forest left in Scotland — mostly in the Highlands. This is because people cleared the woods so they could keep **grazing** animals on the land.

← This map shows the location of the Grampian Mountains. The steepest areas have the darkest pink tint.

Wild salmon live in the sea for most of their life. Many salmon swim into the rivers and lochs in the Grampian Mountains to lay their eggs. They move up rivers against the flow of water to small pools. Salmon return to the same pools where they hatched from eggs themselves.

↑ The Grampian Mountains are cloaked in snow for several months each year.

Native Caledonian Forest trees are Scots pine and juniper. Scots pine is a **conifer** with reddish bark and long needle-leaves. Juniper is a conifer that has **cones** like berries. On the woodland floor shrubs, such as bilberry and heather, and other plants, such as mosses, are common.

Pine wildlife

Several types of animal thrive in Grampian pinewoods. Scottish crossbills are small red birds only found in Britain. They use their beaks to twist open Scots pine cones to get at the **seeds** inside. Red squirrels are red with tufted ears and bushy tails. They use their sharp front teeth to bite open cones. Pine martens are long, chocolate-brown **mammals** with white or cream bellies. They make a den in a hollow tree or on a rocky ledge. Female pine martens give birth in the den to three or four young in spring. By summer, the young leave the den and search for food with their mother.

Get this!

The tallest mountain in the British Isles — Ben Nevis, 1344 metres — is one of the Grampian Mountains.

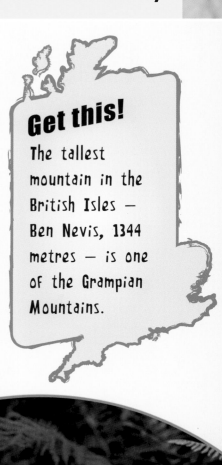

This pine marten is looking for food. Pine martens eat bird eggs, beetles, voles and fungi on the ground and can even hunt red squirrels through trees. ➜

Under threat

Many mountain and hill **habitats** are precious and can be destroyed over time if they are not managed carefully. They are threatened in many different ways, usually by people.

The trouble with tourism

Tourism is important for people in **upland** areas. For example, visitors spend money in local shops and help keep people in work. However, uplands suffer in several ways when people visit. Too many walkers, runners and cyclists **erode** thin upland soil as they move across it. This means there is less soil for plants to live on. People may drop litter, which looks bad and can harm animals. For example, voles may be trapped and die in glass bottles. Walkers can trample and destroy unusual plants, such as orchids, or their dogs may chase or frighten ground-nesting birds, such as red grouse.

Burning

Sometimes, fires can be started accidentally by tourists. These fires can spread rapidly and destroy large areas of heath. This happens because if heather is not burnt often enough it gets long, dry and woody. And when it gets dry it becomes easy to burn. To prevent accidental fires landowners regularly burn areas of **moorland** heather.

This path on the Pennine Way in Derbyshire is being worn ever wider by numerous tourists visiting each year. ➔

This is a way of managing it. They also do this so that grouse, which are hunted for sport, can feed on the new leaves that grow from burnt plants. The new heather that grows also provides shelter, food and nest sites for other animals.

Overgrazing

Many upland heaths stay as rich, open habitats because most farmers control when and for how long their animals **graze** there. However, overgrazing – when too many animals are allowed to graze an area at once – can create large areas of rough grass tussocks and bracken. Overgrazing stops other less tough plants from flowering and surviving. It often reduces the amount of cover for small animals, so **predators** can catch them more easily.

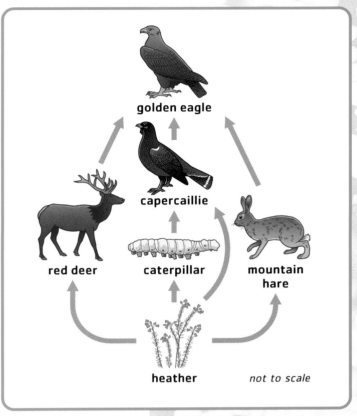

golden eagle

capercaillie

red deer   caterpillar   mountain hare

heather   *not to scale*

↑ This is a diagram of a mountain food web. A food web is a series of living things that eat or are eaten by each other. All food webs start with a plant.

Capercaillies

Capercaillies are the largest type of grouse in Britain. Their original habitat is **native** pine woodland, but capercaillies also live in **conifer plantations**. Deer can cause a lot of damage to trees. People protect plantations from deer by putting fences around them. Capercaillies are now threatened because of these fences. At **breeding** time, males sheltering at the edge of plantations make deep calls to attract females. Many females fly into the fences and die.

Conservation and protection

Uplands in the British Isles are protected and cared for by many different people and organizations. National Parks are large areas of hills and mountains that are looked after to protect wild plants and animals and attract visitors. The largest National Park in England is the Lake District. It covers 2292 square kilometres (885 square miles) and 120 people work there, from information centre workers to wardens. Wardens protect uplands in different ways. For example, they stop areas from becoming too **eroded** by controlling where tourists walk. They also check that landowners do not burn heather at the wrong time of year.

Get this!

It is illegal to burn heather between 15 April and 31 August each year when many ground-nesting birds still have their young.

Wardens sometimes teach groups of schoolchildren about upland plants and animals. They also tell them how to help conserve wild upland areas. These children are in Gwynedd, Wales. ➔

Conservation groups

Many conservation groups raise money to help protect uplands. The National Trust buys up land and protects it with its own wardens. It gets its money from people who join the group because they want to help conserve Britain. In 1998, the National Trust raised £3 million in just two months to buy part of Snowdonia. The British Trust for Conservation organizes groups of **volunteers** to help plant trees, for example, or mend eroded paths.

Taking care

Tourists can help protect mountains and hills in various ways. They should stick to paths, not drop litter, never start fires, close gates behind them and control their dogs. The British Mountaineering Club advises its members to avoid climbing in places where rare wildlife may be affected, such as mountain-top ledges.

Farmers can protect hill land by controlling burning and preventing overgrazing. But if farmers keep more sheep in an upland field to feed, they can sell more sheep at market. The British government sometimes pays farmers to keep the numbers of **grazing** animals on hilly areas low – and therefore protect wild animals and plants.

Grazing can also help uplands, as long as it is carefully managed. For example, bracken, a type of fern, is spreading up the sides of the Malvern Hills, covering areas where many different flowering plants formerly grew. By allowing sheep to graze on the hills, landowners are reducing the amount of bracken and encouraging other plants to grow.

↑ Any visitor to British mountains should stick to the marked paths. This keeps soil erosion to particular areas. It means mountain plants and animals in other areas are not disturbed.

Ospreys are uncommon fish-eating **birds of prey**. They nest in pine forests in Scotland. Some people try to steal the eggs of rare birds to sell to collectors. Wardens at the Loch Garten nature reserve keep a close eye on osprey nests to make sure they are not disturbed.

Glossary

adapt when plants or animals have special features that help them live in their habitat. For example, ducks have webbed feet to help them swim.

bacteria tiny organisms that live in air, water or soil. Some bacteria help to rot dead plants and animals.

bird of prey bird that hunts animals for food

bog area of permanently wet spongy ground, formed especially by decaying plants

breed when a male and female animal have babies

broadleaved tree with large flat leaves and hard wood

camouflage special pattern or colour that helps an animal hide

cone dry woody fruit containing seeds on conifers

conifer type of tree with cones and needle-shaped leaves that is usually not deciduous

erosion wearing away of soil and rocks by wind or water

exposed open to strong winds, rain and cold

fungi group of living things, some of which look like plants, that cannot make their own food by photosynthesis. They include mushrooms and toadstools.

graze eat grass and other plants

habitat type of place where a plant or animal lives. There are many different habitats in the world, such as a mountain habitat or a rainforest habitat.

hibernation special sleep used by some animals to avoid the bad weather and scarce food in winter. Hibernating animals slow down their breathing and heart rate so they can survive using less energy.

insect small six-legged animals, which, when adult, have bodes divided into three sections: head, thorax (chest) and abdomen (stomach)

larvae baby animals, such as insects, that look very different from adults

mammal type of animal with some hair. Female mammals can give birth to live young, which they feed on their own milk.

mate what a male and female animal do to make new offspring (young)

moorland wet areas of upland heath

native original inhabitant of a place

nectar sweet liquid made by some flowering plants to attract animal pollinators

nutrients kinds of chemicals found in soil or in food that nourish plants and animals

organism living thing

peat soil made of vegetable matter found in swamps. When dried it is used as fuel.

photosynthesis process by which plants make their own food using water, air and energy from sunlight

plantation woodland planted and managed by people

pollination when pollen from the male part of a plant combines with an ovule (egg) in the female part of a plant to form seeds

predator animal that catches and eats other animals

prey animal caught by predators to eat

rodent type of mammal with long tail, clawed feet and teeth for gnawing. Mice and rats are rodents.

seed most plants produce seeds that can grow into new plants

species type of organisms. Members of one species cannot usually breed with a different species.

upland area of high land on a mountain or hill

volunteer person who offers to do something of his own free will

wax shiny, waterproof substance

weathering breaking up of soil or rock when exposed

zone area containing similar things. For example, different plants grow in different zones up a mountain.